Turkish Van Cats

A Complete Turkish Van Cat Owner's Guide

Turkish Van Cats General Info, Purchasing, Showing, Care, Cost, Diet, Health, Supplies, Grooming, Training and More Included!

By Lolly Brown

Copyrights and Trademarks

All rights reserved. No part of this book may be reproduced or transformed in any form or by any means, graphic, electronic, or mechanical, including photocopying, recording, taping, or by any information storage retrieval system, without the written permission of the author.

This publication is Copyright ©2022 NRB Publishing, an imprint. Nevada. All products, graphics, publications, software and services mentioned and recommended in this publication are protected by trademarks. In such instance, all trademarks & copyright belong to the respective owners. For information consult www.NRBpublishing.com

Disclaimer and Legal Notice

This product is not legal, medical, or accounting advice and should not be interpreted in that manner. You need to do your own due-diligence to determine if the content of this product is right for you. While every attempt has been made to verify the information shared in this publication, neither the author, neither publisher, nor the affiliates assume any responsibility for errors, omissions or contrary interpretation of the subject matter herein. Any percceived slights to any specific person(s) or organization(s) are purely unintentional.

We have no control over the nature, content and availability of the web sites listed in this book. The inclusion of any web site links does not necessarily imply a recommendation or endorse the views expressed within them. We take no responsibility for, and will not be liable for, the websites being temporarily unavailable or being removed from the internet.

The accuracy and completeness of information provided herein and opinions stated herein are not guaranteed or warranted to produce any particular results, and the advice and strategies, contained herein may not be suitable for every individual. Neither the author nor the publisher shall be liable for any loss incurred as a consequence of the use and application, directly or indirectly, of any information presented in this work. This publication is designed to provide information in regard to the subject matter covered.

Neither the author nor the publisher assume any responsibility for any errors or omissions, nor do they represent or warrant that the ideas, information, actions, plans, suggestions contained in this book is in all cases accurate. It is the reader's responsibility to find advice before putting anything written in this book into practice. The information in this book is not intended to serve as legal, medical, or accounting advice.

Foreword

The Turkish Van cat is popular for various reasons. From its amazing coat, to its lovable personality traits and swimming abilities, many cat keepers who own this breed are surely filled with love and amusement all day long. While all cat breeds are unique in their appearance and characteristics, no cat is quite as unique as the Turkish Van. This breed is one of the oldest domestic cats to date. They made their way to Europe and America around 1955 and 1982 respectively. Turkish Van cats came from Eastern Turkey region particularly in the lake area called Lake Van hence the name. Today, they are one of the most recognized cat breed in the world and are beloved by many cat keepers worldwide.

What's quite surprising for most keepers especially the newbies is that Turkish van cats are quite similar to owning a dog. This is because unlike other cats, Turkish Vans can walk on leashes, play fetch, climb and also swim! They are a clever breed and highly trainable just like dog breeds. However, they don't prefer to be cuddled all the time because they are not a lap cat.

If you're the type of person who wants to teach a cat on how to do tricks, then this is perhaps the best breed for you. You'll soon find them up above your book shelf or on the highest point of the room. They are also the kind of breed that is very independent and has a mind of their own. Turkish Van cats are talkative and very vocal in nature. They love to swim because their body structure is built in a way that makes swimming an easy task for them so don't be surprise if you find them on the pool or joins you on your bathtub. There'll never be a dull moment when you're with this awesome cat breed.

This book will guide you on how you to properly care for your pet Turkish Van cat. You'll get to learn more about their history, biological information, training and grooming needs, health, and the proper diet to keep your pet healthy and happy!

Table of Contents

Introduction 1
Chapter One: The Rare and Treasured Cat 2
    Personality 4
    Living With Turkish Van Cats 5
    The Piebald Gene 7
    Are Other "Van Cats" Related to the Turkish Van? 9
    Pros and Cons of Owning a Turkish Van 11
        Pros 11
        Cons 14
Chapter Two: The Turkish Van Cat Factor 16
    The Turkish Van Cat Factor! 17
    Owning Kittens vs. Adults 22
        Pros and Cons of Owning a Kitten 22
        Pros and Cons of Owning Adult Cats 24
    Travelling with your Pet 26
        Tips on Travelling with Your Pet 29
Chapter Three: The Keeper's Corner 32
    Acquiring a Cat in the United States 33
    Acquiring a Cat in the United Kingdom 35
    Choosing a Reputable Cat Breeder 36
    Things to Keep in Mind When Acquiring a Turkish Van 39

Chapter Four: Bringing Home Your Turkish Van Cat 42

    Bringing Home Your Newfound Pet 43

    Setting Up the Right Environment for Your Turkish Van Cat 45

    Create an Enriching Home for Your Cat 50

    Introducing Your Turkish Van to Other Household Pets 55

Chapter Five: Supplies and Nutrition for Turkish Van Cats 58

    Kitty Essentials 60

    Nutritional Needs of Cats 66

    Feeding Requirements 68

    Homemade Meal Options 70

Chapter Six: Official Breed Standard and Showing Your Cat 72

    Official Breed Standard 73

    Showing Your Turkish Van 84

    Training Your Turkish Van for Show 85

Chapter Seven: Health Care for Turkish Van Cats 88

    Vaccines and Vet Exams 89

    Spaying and Neutering 91

    Grooming Your Turkish Van 92

    Glossary of Cat Terms 94

Index 100

Photo Credits 108

References 110

Introduction

The Turkish Van is an ancient breed that is quite rare to find in the United States back then. This cat breed originated in the southwest and central Asia which today is known as the southwest Soviet Union and eastern regions of Turkey. The word "Van" is a term in these regions that are usually given to villages and town including lakes. This is why it's not a surprise that this breed was coined as the "Vancat" by natives of that particular region in Turkey.

The Turkish cats were first brought to the United Kingdom in 1955, and it was only later that the name is

Introduction

changed to Turkish Van in order to avoid confusion with another cat breed which is the Turkish Angora. Although the breed has an ancient background, it's a newcomer to the U.S. when it arrived for the first time in 1982. Turkish Van cats are very rare even in regions where it has been known to originate in for centuries. This is the reason why they are considered 'treasures' in their homeland and are not readily available to be exported to other countries like other cat breeds.

The Turkish Van breed was brought by European crusaders who recently came from the Middle East, and for many centuries, these cats have been known by various names such as the Russian long – hair, and the White Ringtail. Turkish Van cats are usually mistaken with another similarly looking breed known as the Turkish Angora. However, in reality, they are very distinct breeds that originated in the distant regions of Turkey. And if you happen to see both of this breed together, you will immediately notice their differences particularly in their coat, size and body structure.

Introduction

The coloration of the Turkish Van is a white and semi – longhaired coat with colored markings that are restricted to the breed's tail and head. This coloration was passed on from the ancestral breed and carried by the piebald gene. Over the centuries, there are other piebald cat breeds that have been developed to achieve similar van – patterned markings after the Turkish Van cat sported theirs. Their coat has cashmere – like texture that is water – resistant but they don't have an undercoat. Indeed, the Turkish Van cats have very interesting coats making them more appealing.

Another magnificent feature of this breed is their ability to swim. They are known to love water which is why in their homeland they are also known as the "Swimming Cats."

The Turkish Van cat takes about 3 to 5 years to reach full maturity. They grow into a large and agile breed that's also very smart and well – mannered. They make very rewarding home companions and they will surely keep you entertained all day long. The Turkish Van cats require little

Introduction

grooming because their unique coat is not prone to matting compared to other cat breeds.

If you are going to buy a Turkish Van breed, the pricing usually depend on the bloodline and markings of the cat. Champion breeds such as Grand Champion, National Regional, and Distinguished Merit title holders are very expensive. The Distinguished Merit title is given to a dam (mother cat) that produced 5 CFA grand champion breeds; or a sire (father cat) that produced 15 CFA grand champion offspring. Most Turkish Van breeders make the kittens for sale once they reach around 12 to 16 weeks of age. After around 12 weeks, the kittens have developed physical and social stability and they've already had their basic inoculations. They are now ready to be introduced into a new environment, for show competitions, or be transported wherever their new owners reside.

According to the CFA, the essential elements for maintaining a long, healthy and happy life for the Turkish Van cat breed includes neutering/ spaying, providing

Introduction

adequately for their basic needs – food, shelter, husbandry, health care etc., and of course time, attention and love.

In the next few chapters, you'll get to learn everything you need to know about one of the most ancient and rare cat breeds in history – the Turkish Van Cats.

Introduction

Chapter One: The Rare and Treasured Cat

The Turkish Van is a large – sized cat breed that weighs around 7 to 10 pounds. Males weigh between 10 and 12 pounds while females weigh between 7 to 10 pounds. It is a very intelligent and active animal breed that's also not prone to genetic issues. One of the most distinct characteristic of the Turkish Van is his athletic prowess both on land and water! Unlike most cats that run at the sight of water, the Turkish Van is fond of swimming though it doesn't necessarily mean that he loves to take a bath. Nevertheless, he earned the name "The Swimming Cat" because of their swimming abilities.

Chapter One: The Rare and Treasured Cat

The soft – textured water – resistant silky coat of the Turkish Van is the reason why it has a strong capability to enjoy water – related activities. You can expect this cat to be immersed in water for long periods of time and still come out relatively dry. Make sure to keep an eye out whenever your cat is swimming in the pool or taking a dip right in your own bathtub to avoid any mishaps.

Another distinct physical feature in their coat is the Van – pattern. You'll notice that the breed sports almost an all – white colored body coat with a coloring on its head and tail (some Van cats possess a small roundish mark where their shoulder blades meet). Other colors include brown and red. The unique Van – pattern occurs because of the so – called piebald gene which is a trait that appears not just in animals but also humans. This is large un – pigmented areas of the body which is why the cat appears to be mostly white in color. Apart from the unique markings, the Turkish Van cat's squirrel – like bushy tail also adds to their distinct looking appearance.

Chapter One: The Rare and Treasured Cat

Another distinct physical feature is their different eye colors. A Turkish Van cat may sport 2 blue eyes, 2 amber eyes, or one of each which is a trait that's not uncommon to the breed.

Personality

Most Turkish Van keepers describe the breed as playful, very active, and a fun – loving companion. The cat requires lots of time and attention from their owners even if they are not the lap cat type of breed. The Turkish Van is perfect for keepers who have lots of love and time to share with their furry companion. According to The International Cat Association, Turkish Van cats are jumpers. This is because they possess very powerful back legs making it easy for them to climb on top of shelves, doors, or even trees! Expect them to literally be on top of everything as they take pleasure in seeing the world around them from a bird's eye view. Apart from that, they can also be trained to play fetch, chase toys, or do somersaults and other tricks which is why they are often compared to owning a dog.

Chapter One: The Rare and Treasured Cat

Living With Turkish Van Cats

The Turkish Van can get along with other cat breeds and even dog breeds. However, you need to make sure that they have a proper introduction or sort of a 'meet – and – greet' before you leave them alone with your other household pets or even with young children (if any). It's best that you supervise them whenever they're interacting or playing with kids and other animal breeds.

Turkish Van cats like to be cuddled but not for a long time. As mentioned earlier, they are loving cats but they don't tolerate people petting them or tugging at their tails. It's always best to train and socialize them at a young age since this breed is very curious and intelligent. Make sure to also provide them with physically and mentally stimulating toys as well as regular exercise.

The breed can also be quite mischievous due to its curiosity and high energy. They can sometime be a bit careless especially when it comes to ornaments or other things around the house. Since they love to jump and climb,

Chapter One: The Rare and Treasured Cat

you would want to keep your household items safe because your Van cat will surely knock them over. To keep them from doing such things, it's best to buy your cat with plenty of toys or create a Do – It – Yourself toys so that you can take their attention away from your valuables and also gets to spend quality time with them.

The Turkish Van cats do not reach full maturity until they reach around 3 to 5 years. They are also low shedders and low maintenance since they possess a single and semi - long coat that has a cashmere – like texture. You need to ensure that they receive regular grooming routine such as brushing of teeth, combing (can be done just once a week since they possess a coat that's not prone to matting), claw trimming and the likes. They don't require regular bathing and they are also less allergenic. They are very rare to find so make sure to truly care for them and make them part of the family once you've finally acquire this rare breed. They can live for around 13 to 17 years and the breed is also recognized by various cat organizations around the world including the Cat Fanciers Association (CFA), The International Cat Association (TICA), the American Cat

Chapter One: The Rare and Treasured Cat

Fanciers Association (ACFA), the Federacion International Feline (FIFe), and the World Cat Federation (WCF).

The Piebald Gene

Contrary to what newbie keepers think, Turkish Vans are not white cats. They only possess large patches of white but in reality they are colored cats. The white patches just become sort of the dominant color which is why most people think that it's a white – colored cat splash with other colors on the tail and head. This is due to piebald gene which also known as the piebald white spotting gene or white spotting gene. The piebald gene passed on from the ancestral breed of the Turkish Van cats is responsible for the white – patch pattern on their coats as well as the colored marking on their faces and tail.

You can also randomly find spots of colors that are small, medium and large in size all over their body as well as their legs. According to official standards of the breed, one or more random markings that are around 20% of the body are allowed. Random markings shouldn't be

Chapter One: The Rare and Treasured Cat

of a number or size that detracts the van – pattern as this could make the breed appear bi – color. A symmetrical pattern of head markings, divided by the color white up to the level of the ears' front edge is preferred. A Turkish Van cat with total absence of color on its tail or head calls for a disqualification same with a cat that has a color in excess of 20% of its body.

Genetically speaking, a breeder can produce a solid white color van cat but this kind of Turkish Van will not be allowed for showing. Most breeders strive to produce offspring that has a full colored tail, little to no body spots, and colored markings on the head.

The following are the standard Turkish Van coat colors:

Solid and White Colors
- Red
- Black
- Blue
- Cream

Chapter One: The Rare and Treasured Cat

Tabby and White Colors

- Red Tabby
- Cream Tabby
- Brown Tabby
- Blue Tabby

Parti - color and White Colors:

- Tortoiseshell
- Dilute Tortoiseshell
- Brown Patched Tabby
- Blue Patched Tabby

Are Other "Van Cats" Related to the Turkish Van?

Should you decide to sign up for your Turkish Van cat for show, you might start to wonder if there are other breeds such as the Van Persians, Van Cornish Rex, and Van Maine Coons are related to the Turkish Van cat breed since they exhibit similar coat colorings and patterns. Well, the answer is no. The other van cat breeds aforementioned are simply Persian cat breeds, Maine Coons cat breeds, and Cornish Rex cat breeds that only

Chapter One: The Rare and Treasured Cat

exhibit van – patterns. Perhaps a more correct designation for such breeds exhibiting similar coat patterns should be Van – Patterned Persian, Van – Patterned Cornish Rex, and Van – Patterned Maine Coon.

In addition the 3 cat breeds aforementioned, other breeds that may have the van pattern include the following:

- American Shorthair
- American Curl
- Devon Rex
- Norwegian Forest Cat
- British Shorthair
- Exotic Rex
- Selkirk Rex
- Oriental Rex

Chapter One: The Rare and Treasured Cat

Pros and Cons of Owning a Turkish Van

Acquiring such a rare and 'treasured' cat breed is a huge responsibility as this will entail bringing up another 'family member' in your life. You will have another obligation because you need to take care of this breed for a long time. However, the Turkish Van is a great companion because they will surely keep you entertained and will also give you love and affection. Nevertheless, you need to know both the positive and negative traits about the Turkish Van cat before you finally buy this breed because the last thing you want is to put this ancient and rare breed up for adoption.

Pros

They can easily adjust to their environment: The Turkish Van easily adapts to change and it will surely enjoy their life as long as you provide them with all their basic needs. If you are out of town, the cat will not panic even if you will let other people take care of it for the mean time. They are very independent and can handle themselves to any situation.

Chapter One: The Rare and Treasured Cat

They can get along with kids and other household pets: Some cat breeds can be quite unfriendly especially when it comes to children. Fortunately not the Turkish Van. They can get along with kids and other household pets as long as you supervise them and properly introduce them to each other. Make sure to teach your kids on how to properly hold or pet the cat to avoid any mishaps. You can your Turkish Van love to play with kids, spend their free time with them, and knows how to deal with it even if the kids gets all over them. Another plus for this breed is that they will not get too aggressive even if they are already irritated though they may tend to jump to get away from too much handling.

Their coats are luxurious and easy to maintain: The main advantage of owning a Turkish Van cat breed is that they sport a luxurious soft coat that's water – resistant, not prone to matting and easy to maintain. They are very low shedders and you won't find their hair scattered all over your furniture unlike other cat breeds. Its coat does not require too much grooming and you only need to do some minor brushing at least once a week to maintain its silky semi – long coat.

Chapter One: The Rare and Treasured Cat

They are highly trainable and very clever: Turkish Van cats are very intelligent. They love adults, kids, and also instructions. This breed can be taught how to fetch stuff, and do various cool tricks. They love to follow instructions and knows how to do things right. However, if you are not firm with your actions especially on the instance that they did something undesirable, the cat may learn that you are not the authority that they need to follow.

They are lovable and an affectionate companion: Turkish Van cats love their parent owners. This breed loves to spend quality time with their keepers and other household pets. You can sleep next to it, cuddle them a bit, play with them along with your kids, and be close to you. They will not run away from you if you give them love and attention. It is very entertaining to watch your cat go about and play around in different positions. They will jump on you just to show you their love!

Chapter One: The Rare and Treasured Cat

They are low maintenance and are not prone to major illnesses: Just provide your Turkish Van with a litter box, water, and food and he/she will do just fine. You can go out for a weekend and you do not need a pet sitter. In addition, they are quite healthy and are not prone to genetic or hereditary illnesses.

Cons

They are expensive and could be hard to find: Turkish Van cat breeds aren't as rare as they were before but they could still be hard to find depending on your location. Make sure to check your local cat organization to get information on where you can legitimately acquire a Turkish Van breed. Expect the price to be more expensive if the color or Van – pattern markings are quite unique. You will possibly pay more if the Turkish Van is from championship lineage.

They can be hyperactive and can ruin your furniture: By default, having a cat means dealing with different furniture being scratched and in the case of Turkish Van cat your ornaments will get toppled down since they love to jump!

Chapter One: The Rare and Treasured Cat

Make sure to provide them with a separate scratching post and provide physically and mentally stimulating toys to keep boredom at bay otherwise your pet will not have any outlet and this will cause them to misbehave inside the house.

Chapter Two: The Turkish Van Cat Factor

Do you want a rare cat that stands out? Then look no further because the Turkish Van is just the pet you are looking for! There are so many reasons why people are attracted to the Turkish Van breed and those reasons doesn't end with their remarkably distinct appearance. This feline, with its great disposition and extreme intelligence, has is becoming more popular than ever because of its well – mannered yet fun – loving personality. Homes with existing feline - friendly pets and young children have notably welcomed the Turkish Van with hardly any issues due to its

Chapter Two: The Turkish Van Cat Factor

even - temperedness. Families with children get to enjoy family routines which include and involve the feline being raised alongside them. The Turkish Van has been a great addition of inspiration and joy to both newbie and experienced keepers who have discovered the rewards of living with one.

The Turkish Van Cat Factor!

The Turkish Van breed warms up easily to people so be wary that you not let them out of the house without a leash. Yes, they can be highly trainable to walk with one just like a dog! And if you give them the right amount of space and time they will crawl up to your lap and contentedly curl up with you but not for a long time! Keep in mind; they don't enjoy too much petting. It is a cool feline who is not at all bothered to be around strangers or be in new places. True to its feline nature, the Turkish Van reserves making judgments about anything or anyone until it has studied, surveyed and observed everything and everyone. But just a bit of reminder, they love attention from its owners but only thrive on occasional hugs and slight petting.

Chapter Two: The Turkish Van Cat Factor

Once the consensus is in and it determines you to be of no threat to itself, the Van cat will have no qualms in letting you feel how valuable you are. These breeds of cats are deeply devoted and openly affectionate to their human families. This breed is a sweet companion to all the members of the family and will be glad to welcome you at the door when you return home or jump at you! Cats are keenly sensitive toward each of their human family's mood and this feline trait has been discussed to extents amongst feline owner as positive traits of the Turkish Van. This feline breed will sense the change in the emotions of its human family and would seemingly mirror the caregiver's inner workings.

Contrary to what most people think, Turkish Van cat aren't stubborn as long as you patiently train them. They are quite adept to understanding human commands and instructions since they are a clever breed. With enough socialization training through repeated human exposure they are able to understand and learn tricks they are taught.

Chapter Two: The Turkish Van Cat Factor

Find a favored toy which it can manage to carry in its jaws, show it to your pet and throw it a fair distance just like playing fetch with a dog. Do it often enough and observe your pet Turkish Van fetch the toy. The Turkish Van is a very social and vocal cat that has no problems being around new places and people. Generally, cats can get pretty skittish around strange humans and new environments, but not this one. It manages to adjust quite well in new situations so it is the perfect companion to take with you on a routine shopping trip or perhaps an extended vacation.

Turkish Van cats are actively playful and can also get quite occupied on whatever activity they are in at the moment, just like most felines. Just watching them at play will make your heart melt into mush. Call out to them so they get used to their names and wait for them to look into your eyes and be swept away. The felines create really strong bonds with their humans so it is no wonder that feline aficionados talk about this rare and treasured cat breed.

Chapter Two: The Turkish Van Cat Factor

You will eventually see how easily your Turkish Van integrates itself to your family with no problems. Keep in mind though, that if you have young children in the house, training will also need to be given to your kids on how to respectfully handle felines. Turkish Van cats are known jumpers so make sure to supervise them when playing to avoid any mishaps. The measure of trust it has is readily shared for the people it holds dear. In fact, they are such a trusting sort that it would even eagerly greet guests at the door when they sense company!

When it comes to getting along with other pets, like most felines they will hardly ever meow at other cats and might also get along with dog breeds provided of course that you introduce them or better yet raised them together. If your pet tries to communicate with you, consider yourself lucky because that means they need something from you! You will in time be able to realize what it is trying to say to you.

Chapter Two: The Turkish Van Cat Factor

When it comes to mealtimes expect your pet to get excited, especially when it senses that you are about to feed him. You can train your Turkish Van cat to a certain extent since this breed is an independent thinker. You will soon notice that your pet understand your simple commands and respond by head butting your hand, curl up around your feet or plop itself where you are seated.

When it comes to staying outdoors or indoors, Turkish Van cats are quite a rare breed, you may want to keep them safe and secure for a number of reasons:

- They are an attractive sort and with their friendly nature you might just lose one of them to a stranger if they get picked up by a random person.

- You want to steer clear of feral animals which may infect it with disease and illness.

- You want to keep them safe from vicious attacks.

- You want to keep them away from road traffic which may result to accidents.

Chapter Two: The Turkish Van Cat Factor

Owning Kittens vs. Adults

Now that you have already made up your mind in buying a Turkish Van Cat, the next step is to decide whether you're going to acquire a kitten or an adult Turkish Van. Most people prefer purchasing kittens, while some settle for adult cats. Whatever your choice may be, the level of care and attention is still the same.

Kittens and adult cats have their own advantages and disadvantages. They both have their own needs and wants so the best thing to do is to know what these needs or wants are before you decide what you will settle on. In this section, you will learn the difference between acquiring a kitten and an adult cat.

Pros and Cons of Owning a Kitten

Kittens in general are cute, charming, and need lots of care and attention. It can be compared to raising a toddler. It's a much bigger responsibility if you choose to acquire a kitten because you will need to train them, provide them

Chapter Two: The Turkish Van Cat Factor

with the vaccines they need, and socialize them well enough so that they will grow up to be well – mannered adult cats.

There could be a lot more responsibility when you acquire a kitten but it will surely be a rewarding experience because you will get to see him/ her grow, you'll be a part of your cat's life, and will become more bonded as the years go by.

Kittens are easier to train and socialize, whether you will train it to use a litter box or teach them various tricks. They are also less prone to trouble as they will not get tangled in cods, fall from high places, or be as curious as an adult cat. Kittens are generally easier to introduce to people, fellow cats, or other household pets. Having kittens can also be beneficial to your health and emotional well - being. It can lower your blood pressure and cholesterol. Getting kittens could teach you and your little children about daily responsibility, because there are a lot of things you need to take care of kittens.

Chapter Two: The Turkish Van Cat Factor

In addition to this, kittens can help you in your social life as they can pave the way in establishing new connections with fellow pet owners within your area.

As for the disadvantages, if you get a very young kitten, you may need to bottle feed it. You will also need to get all the vaccines and booster shots throughout its first year which can be both expensive and time – consuming.

Pros and Cons of Owning Adult Cats

Acquiring an adult Turkish Van cat is has its own advantages and disadvantages. Some keepers prefer getting a more matured cat because most of them are already house – trained and you will also skip out on all the vaccines and "kitty issues." On the other hand, some people do not want this because there could be behavioural problems since somebody else raised them up. If you are still thinking of acquiring an adult cat make sure to consider the following pros and cons:

Chapter Two: The Turkish Van Cat Factor

First of all, you can be sure that what you're going to get is a Turkish Van breed since adult cats are already fully developed. You can see the exact the body type or body structure, the eye colors, and their very distinct coat. You can already see their behaviour and temperament such as how active or vocal they can be, how much attention they need from you, or how they interact with other pets and people since the cat has already developed a certain type of personality. Don't worry because an adult cat can still bond with you just like a kitten. Your adult cat could even give more affection because it appreciates you for taking them in.

As for the disadvantages, you may be getting a cat with a behavioural issue and some of them might naturally be wary of strangers since you didn't raised them up in the first place. An adult cat will need to have an adjustment period and will need to recognize you as its leader. You need to completely gain their trust so that you can start bonding with them which can take some time but if you show them your love and affection, you and your adult cat will easy get along.

Chapter Two: The Turkish Van Cat Factor

Travelling with your Pet

Should you plan to travel with your Turkish Van cat then you may need to consider some things before you even pack your pet with you. This holds true especially if you do not want to leave your precious pet with a cat sitter. Taking your pet to another place is time - consuming and complicated process which is why you should do extensive research before you go through the process.

If you are only going away for a short period of time, it's probably best to entrust your pet to your family or friends. Turkish Van cats can be left alone provided that you already trained them and you leave them with all the essentials they need such as food, water, toys, security etc. They are independent and they can survive for quite some time without you. However, if you are going to be gone for a long period of time (few weeks, months to a year) then it's best to bring them along with you. Make sure to consider all of the factors below:

Chapter Two: The Turkish Van Cat Factor

Travelling on a car, plane, or ship

Do you think your pet will be all right to be in a confined place for a long period of time? Make sure to make them comfortable during the whole trip whether it's by car, on the air or at sea. It's also important to check with the airline or shipping line with regards to their regulations on bringing a pet on board.

Some airlines may allow pets to travel in the cabin, only if you have a small cage that will fit under your seat while some airlines will restrict the pet transportation during certain times of the year. Research on the air pressure and temperature in the cargo before you book the flight. It is better for your pet if your flight is direct and has a short travel time. Make sure to research on the specific requirements for the airlines or shipping lines when it comes to transportation of the pet. Before the travel, make sure you have trained your cat to be inside the crate or kennel. You can add toys and pieces of clothing so your pet will be very familiar during the transportation. Last but not least, find pet-friendly airlines or pet – friendly shipping lines before you book your trip.

Chapter Two: The Turkish Van Cat Factor

Quarantine for your pet

This is needed if you are going to travel overseas or if your pet will be placed in the cargo of the plane or ship along with other animals. Consider the risk for your cat's health and take the necessary steps to ensure that your Turkish Van is safe and secure.

Health – Related Threats during Travel

The concern of many countries with pets from overseas is the transmission of certain diseases. They are afraid that avian influenza and rabies might spread from birds to humans. Rabies is the main concern for cats and other household pets which is why you need to present a rabies vaccination to make sure that your cat does not have rabies.

In addition to this, you need to research how long the quarantine is for the country or place that you will go to. Keep in mind that you will not be with your pet during this quarantine period. A problem for this is the expensiveness of the quarantine, which could last up to six months. Aside from this, there are strict import requirements for pet imports for specific countries.

Chapter Two: The Turkish Van Cat Factor

You also need to think about the possible health threats for your pets when it travels overseas. There is no specific immunization against the avian flu or other dangerous disease or parasites that may affect your pet.

Tips on Travelling with Your Pet

Tip #1: Make sure you have the money to spend for travelling costs. If you travel with your pet overseas, make sure you list down all the costs you need before you book your flight. You may need to pay for the vaccinations and health certificates before the flight which could be very expense. You need to also keep in mind that the cost of traveling with your pet will increase overtime.

Tip #2: Cargo or cabin? If you do not want your pet to travel with you in a cabin, you may need to travel it through the cargo. You need to remember that shipping your pet and placing your cat on a cargo could make him or her uncomfortable. Make sure to place him/her on a comfortable kennel and consider all the risk such as pressure on the cargo etc.

Chapter Two: The Turkish Van Cat Factor

Tip #3: Quarantine your pet. Your Turkish Van may need to be quarantined again once you get back to your home country.

These are just some things that you need to remember if you want to travel with your pet. Make sure to weigh the pros and cons before you decide to book a flight. If you think this is too much for you or your pet to handle, then it's probably best to let friends or family members take care of your pet while you're gone.

Chapter Two: The Turkish Van Cat Factor

Chapter Three: The Keeper's Corner

Cats are becoming a staple member of households and even private institutions all over the world, which make the presence of laws governing cat ownership essential. Ultimately, laws are geared towards protecting pets from abuse and neglect as well as protecting the community from animals that may become threatening to the public. As responsible pet owners, it is our duty to be fully informed about them and uphold them. By doing so, we are contributing to a better community not only for our feline friends, but also for ourselves.

Chapter Three: The Keeper's Corner

When it comes to acquiring one, finding a good breeder is what you need to do to be paired with a healthy Turkish Van. Reputable breeders follow a code of ethics prohibiting sales to wholesalers and pet stores. The code they observe and abide outlines the breeder's responsibilities to buyers and their breeds. To find breeders and to get more information about the personality and history of the Turkish Van you can check out cat association websites like the Cat Fanciers Association (CFA), and the American Cat Fanciers Association (ACFA).

This chapter will provide you with information on how you can legally keep this rare and treasured breed as well as some tips on how to find the right breeder.

Acquiring a Cat in the United States

Unlike dog owners, cat owners are not required to obtain a license for their cats across all states in the U.S., except in Rhode Island, where it is mandated. However, there are some municipal ordinances that may require proof of vaccination and identification, particularly in Alabama, where owners are required to have their cat or dog

Chapter Three: The Keeper's Corner

vaccinated yearly to make sure that all pets, owners, and civilians are protected from rabies. This is actually a good measure in the event of cat bites and scratches. Remember, cats can be infected with rabies, too, so if you haven't yet, bring your pet to a vet and ask to be scheduled for vaccination as soon as possible.

Cats are not required to wear collars in the U.S. as it is believed to go against their nature. It is, however, good for cats get used to wearing collars for these reasons: (1) So they can be easily identified – in the event that your cat accidentally gets out the gate and gets lost, having the owner's contact details on the collar makes is easier for concerned citizens to help out. (2) So that people can be informed of the cat's medical condition. This comes in handy particularly if you're leaving your cat in a pet inn while you're away on a trip. It is highly advisable to have their collar inscribed with any medical conditions they have to ensure that your cat will be properly fed and cared for. Same goes for when your cat goes missing; people who found it would immediately know that the cat needs special medical attention.

Chapter Three: The Keeper's Corner

To ensure that your cat's collar won't interfere with its movements or cause injuries, always check if it is properly secured on the neck. If you can slip two fingers between the collar and the kitty's neck, then it's all good! A collar that's too tight might cause irritation, while having it too loose might cause it to get snagged on objects.

For further information regarding licensing requirements and ordinances in your area here are some tips:

- Give your local government a call or simply look up their website
- Ask or check if there are downloadable forms for cat licensing.
- Mail the form to the town hall or hand it over personally. The registration fee may vary across the states.

Acquiring a Cat in the United Kingdom

Since the U.K. has successfully eliminated Rabies in 1922, your cat may be required to undergo a quarantine period as a strict safety measure. They definitely love their feline friends so much that earlier this year, the government pledged to develop more laws to protect kittens from exploitation. This was after discovering that some kittens are being bred in poor conditions and are taken away from their mothers too soon. The new law states that license exemptions for people who repeatedly sell kittens that are bred from non - pedigree cats will be removed, and there will be stricter conditions for breeder licenses to be approved.

Choosing a Reputable Cat Breeder

Selecting the wrong breeder can make or break you as a pet keeper. If you acquire your Turkish Van from an illegitimate source, you may eventually find out that the kitten you got is not even a Turkish Van! Since this breed is expensive, rare and one of a kind, you need to make sure that you only get it from a reputable source. Finding the right breeder is E-V-E-R-Y-T-H-I-N-G.

However, breeders aren't the only source to acquire a Turkish Van cat. You won't usually find a Turkish Van kitten in rescues or shelters but you may still come across

Chapter Three: The Keeper's Corner

both mixed and pedigreed Turkish Van breeds there. There are many reasons why adult pets end up in shelters and rescue facilities like divorce, death, owners relocated, illness and the list goes on. You might stumble onto good fortune and find the perfect Turkish Van for you and your family. You could also try checking your shelters in your locale or check out pet finder listings.

No matter where you get your Turkish Van pet make sure that there is a written contract with the seller, shelter or rescue group is thorough and details the responsibilities of both parties. If you look up this breed online you will get quite a few hits on breeders selling. It can be daunting to figure out which breeders are reputable and which ones are just in it for the money. Things like convenience, such as ability to pay online, multiple kitten availability at all times, having choices for any kitten "readily available" are some of the red flags that would identify a shady "breeder" because after all Turkish Van is a rare breed.

Select a breeder who has completed the health certifications required to screen out genetic health problems

Chapter Three: The Keeper's Corner

to the fullest extent possible. You need to get in touch with a breeder who raises and keeps the kittens in their home. Isolated kittens can become skittish, fearful and may be difficult to socialize later. Run away from breeders who only seem bent in how fast they can pass on and unload a kitten on you. Turn your back on those who are more concerned about whether your credit card will go through. You also want to be able to pay a visit to their home facilities and check out with your own eyes how they interact and how the kittens respond to them.

Reputable breeders will have no problems welcoming you into their premises. Buying from a website with no possibility of seeing the pets in action leaves you very little guarantee that you will be getting what was agreed upon. This is why we highly recommend that you check the cat personally and not just through online photos or videos.

You can also pay a visit and discuss this with your veterinarian. They can usually point you to the direction of a breed rescue organization, a reputable breeder, or other trustworthy sources of healthy kittens. Put as much effort

Chapter Three: The Keeper's Corner

into researching your kitten as you would into picking out a new car or other big ticket purchases. Doing so will save you money in the long run. Depending on what pet you are looking for, you may have to sit it out for six months or more before the right kittens are available. So be patient. Reputable breeders typically will not hand over kittens to new people until the kittens are between twelve and sixteen weeks of age.

Things to Keep in Mind When Acquiring a Turkish Van

Unhealthy catteries and disreputable breeders can be difficult to identify from reliable operations. There is no absolute guarantee that you won't be purchasing an ill kitten. Therefore asking the right questions, researching the breed so you understand what to expect and visiting the facilities to determine the conditions and see the animals for yourself is vital to lessen the chances of heartache, disappointment and wasted finances.

Make sure that you have a clean contract with your source (clearly stating the responsibilities of both breeder and buyer), or you have the necessary permits if you're

Chapter Three: The Keeper's Corner

going to acquire one from a rescue group or shelter. Whether you get a kitten or adult Turkish Van, you will need to take your kitten or cat to the veterinarian right after adoption. Your veterinarian will be able to see problems with the feline's health, and would work with you to create a preventive regimen which will help avoid countless health issues.

Prior to buying a kitten, think about whether a mature Turkish Van might be a better choice for you and your lifestyle. Kittens are buckets full of fun but they also entail a load of work and could be somewhat destructive until they reach a more easy-going state of adulthood.

If you purchase an adult, you would know more about what to expect of the cat in terms of health and personality. Should you consider getting an adult Turkish Van instead of a kitten, ask breeders about buying a retired breeding or a show cat. Check out the previous chapter about the pros and cons of getting a kitten versus an adult cat.

Chapter Three: The Keeper's Corner

Chapter Four: Bringing Home Your Turkish Van Cat

One thing that keeps a cat happy is when it knows that it has a safe and comfortable home. Sometimes though, a cat's curious nature gets it into trouble, creating a hassle both for you and your pet. More mature cats are less likely to be mischievous, while kittens can be a bit trickier to handle. Whatever the size of your home is, you will definitely need to ensure that it is cat - proof and an ideal place for your feline friend to thrive. For sure you've seen tons of entertaining videos all over social media showing a

Chapter Four: Bringing Home Your Turkish Van Cat

tiny cat comfortably sleeping on a mini bed tailor - made for it. Although it looks absolutely adorable, kittens will need more than just cozy sleeping furniture to grow healthy and strong. This chapter will teach you tips and tricks to ensure that your home is ready for the arrival of your Turkish Van cat.

Bringing Home Your Newfound Pet

Bringing home a new pet could be a really special experience for humans, but for cats, it can be quite frightening. For you to be able to help them feel secure and ease their tension, you must first understand why cats are scared when being rehomed. Cats dislike change; for them, a new home means entering new territory, meeting new possible enemies, and encountering new challenges they are not all too familiar with.

Reminders on the ride home and upon arriving

Make sure that your Turkish Van cat is inside a carrier to that it feels safer. Being inside moving vehicles

Chapter Four: Bringing Home Your Turkish Van Cat

may traumatize your cat and cause it much stress that it would start to pant. Panting is a sure sign of anxiety and excessive body heating, so help your cat by keeping it safe inside a well - ventilated cat carrier.

Upon arriving home, it is advised that you let your cat settle into a small room that he can call his early territory. Never force the cat out of the carrier, instead, keep it open and let the cat decide when it is comfortable enough to explore the room. You can have your cat stay in the room for several days so that he gets used to the smells, the sounds, and the sights. Put everything the cat needs in this room, including water and food bowls, litter tray, a few toys to keep him busy, and a comfortable bedding.

You may visit the cat often to see if it is doing fine, but don't stress it out by giving it forced attention or by bringing in new people to the room to pet or play with the cat. Also see to it that your kids don't frighten the cat by entering their haven uninvited. Most cat breeds including the Turkish Van are known to easily adapt to its

Chapter Four: Bringing Home Your Turkish Van Cat

environment, but letting them get used to their new home and new human companions at their own pace will work wonders on your relationship with them.

Setting Up the Right Environment for Your Turkish Van Cat

The environment greatly impacts a cat's overall health and behavior, which is why both the U.S. and U.K. gave reminders and recommendations regarding setting up the right environment for cats, specifically the amount of space needed, the furniture, interaction with other pets and with their owners or other people as well as environmental enrichment including toys and other sensory stimulants. You see, cats are fairly comfortable living on their own, and unlike dogs, they would rather keep a distance to avoid social conflicts.

If you want to set up the right environment for your Turkish Van you need to keep in mind of some things like providing an adequate hiding spot and cat essentials as well as providing a secure playing area that's safe from hazards.

Chapter Four: Bringing Home Your Turkish Van Cat

You have to make sure that there will be hiding spots where your pet can seek refuge and be out of sight at times when it feels stressed or uncomfortable with interactions. You need to provide litter trays, water bowl, and food bowls and make it easily accessible for him/ her especially if you're going to leave your cat. In case you have more than one pet at home, give each pet their own bowls with sufficient supply of food to avoid monopolization.

One of the most common conflicts among cats is guarding their resources from each other, but this may be avoided if you properly allocate their needs. Another important factor is to maximize the vertical space by incorporating elevated and vertical structures inside your house such as climbing poles, shelves, slanted walkways, steps, platforms, cat hammocks, cat trees, resting boxes and the likes since the Turkish Van cats are born climbers and jumpers. You don't need all of the things aforementioned, but having at least some of these in your house is highly essential when living with a cat.

Chapter Four: Bringing Home Your Turkish Van Cat

Felines prefer to spend more time in high places, and having them navigate through these structures will surely be a good exercise and entertainment for them.

You need to also keep containers closed at all times. Kittens are naturally curious and are more likely to climb whatever structures they can. It is a must to keep water containers, garbage cans, and washers & dryers closed at all times as cats can get trapped inside when they fall. Also bear in mind that an open toilet bowl could attract thirsty kittens and may cause drowning, so protect your feline friends by keeping those lids closed.

Of course, a home is not complete if you do not provide comfortable bedding in ideal resting areas. Cats in general enjoy resting in dry and warm areas, usually in corners where they feel more secure. Try to get creative and make cat beds from soft materials such as polyester fleece cloth, so you wouldn't need to spend much on new beds. Studies show that cats that sleep on soft surfaces tend to rest longer than those who sleep on hard surfaces. Another thing

Chapter Four: Bringing Home Your Turkish Van Cat

to keep in mind is to not encourage your cat to nap near hot surfaces like stoves or fireplaces. Although they enjoy resting in warm areas, the fireplace and kitchen top are absolutely not safe places for rest. Gently wake up your cat and move it to a safer spot to remind them that these are not the correct places for napping.

When it comes to essentials, make sure to allot one litter tray for your pet. This is also the ideal allocation if you have several cats at home to ensure good toilet behavior. Remember that cleaning the litter box at least once per day is a must because some cats won't use a tray that's been soiled. You'll find a variety of cat litter in the groceries, and it may take some experimenting to know which type is the most ideal for your cat. Also keep in mind that the locations of the litter box and feeding bowls must be at least 0.50 meters apart and not be interchanged to prevent confusion.

Never leave hazardous and poisonous chemicals exposed. Cats are curious and playful in nature. They will tinker with almost every object they come across with, and

Chapter Four: Bringing Home Your Turkish Van Cat

you wouldn't want you cat suddenly knocking over that bottle of bleach or detergent, or worse, accessing roach and rodent killers. Make sure to keep all dangerous substances secured in cabinets with locks. It's also best to keep away toxic plants at home. Not all plants can be used as catnip, some turn out to be harmful to cats. The most common toxic houseplants are lilies, poinsettia Philodendron, and mistletoe. While garden plants that you should keep your cat away from are daffodils and azaleas.

Do not leave cords and strings dangling. Both adult cats and kittens love chewing and playing with things they can reach or find on the ground. The problem is getting badly entangled in these wires could cause choking. Make sure tape and secure electrical wiring properly. Kittens may think wires are fun to play with, but one wrong bite on this and they'll end up getting badly hurt or electrocuted, and may even cause electrical problems in your home. Avoid problems by checking the house for loose wirings before bringing in a new pet. Don't scatter items like hair ties,

Chapter Four: Bringing Home Your Turkish Van Cat

rubber hands, ribbons, cable ties, rubber erasers, thread, yard, small toy pieces, doll accessories etc.

One way of making sure that your Turkish Van does not play around hazardous materials is to ensure that you provided physically and mentally stimulating cat toys to keep them busy. Turkish Van is known for their intelligence. They easily learn how to open doors, press buttons, and so much more that could get them into trouble. Giving your cat some toys would keep it busy and entertained.

Create an Enriching Home for Your Cat

Once you've got the furniture ready for your pet's arrival, it's now time to know how you can enhance the quality of your cat's life under your watch. Having an ideal house arrangement for pet cat is only the tip of the iceberg because as an owner, you'll need to plan their enrichment activities. Just like humans, pets can get easily bored as well. Playtimes commonly happen after their naps, and this is a good time to stimulate their brain through interaction and physical activities. Check out some tips below:

Chapter Four: Bringing Home Your Turkish Van Cat

Create activities that will physically and mentally stimulate them.

What you can do is to set a little hammock or platform for your cat by the window to excite their eyes. Most cats enjoy looking out windows and observing other people and animals. You can also try letting your Turkish Van cat explore your garden, but only if you are there to supervise him/ her. You wouldn't want to chase them through the neighborhood, so make sure that your gates are closed and never let your cat out of your sight.

Create a stress reliever for your pet.

If you're ever tried listening to classical music, you'd know how effective it can be as a stress reliever. Some say that it has the same effects on cats and other household pets. Although it hasn't been proven, there's no harm in playing soothing music for your Turkish Van cat whenever you see it being hyper active or agitated. Certain types of sounds stimulate their auditory senses. It is highly likely for cats to enjoy music that mimic the rhythm and tonal qualities of purrs. However, the type of music we usually like is

Chapter Four: Bringing Home Your Turkish Van Cat

definitely not the type they enjoy, so be sensitive to your pet before deciding to blast music from your speakers. It hasn't been determined yet whether cats prefer high-pitched or low-pitched sounds. Generally speaking, extremely loud noise could be harmful to your cat.

Provide a catnip.

Catnip is absolutely safe for cats, but feeding them too much of this may cause diarrhea or vomiting. To avoid habituation, it's recommended that you don't give catnip more than once every two to three weeks. Catnip is readily available in pet supplies stores, along with toys stuffed with it. Olfactory stimulation should also be on your priority as cats are born with a highly - developed sense of smell. If you can observe, cats immediately react to certain smells as they get easily attracted by the scent of deliciously - cooked food, and they instantly back away from people, food, or objects whose scent they don't like or recognize. You can help enhance their sense of smell by providing posts or surfaces for scratching. This is especially helpful when you have

Chapter Four: Bringing Home Your Turkish Van Cat

more than one cat at home as cats communicate via their scent glands.

Try natural feeding techniques from time to time.

Meal time is every pet's most loved daily activity. Full and satisfied cats are happy cats as they sleep more soundly and behave better when they are not deprived of a good meal. Since cats like the Turkish Van breed are natural hunters, letting them perform natural feeding behaviors could greatly stimulate their appetite and even their brain functions. In the wild, cats hunt often and they end up eating ten small meals daily.

Create food puzzle toys.

Food puzzle toys enables cat to figure out how to work the object in order to get its food. You can provide treat balls wherein the cat has to roll the ball until cat food falls from the tiny holes all over the ball. You can make one at home by cutting holes on small containers, water bottles, or even toilet paper roles, and then, putting dry food inside

Chapter Four: Bringing Home Your Turkish Van Cat

it. Your cat will surely be intrigued by the sound the treats make when it moves the container.

Another type of food puzzle will not only allow cats to experience natural feeding behaviors is known as foraging feeders. It can also help prevent cats from over indulging that leads to obesity. It mimics the experience of scooping out food from small, difficult spaces, which cats in the wild usually do. You can also play circuit boards which is a type of food puzzle toy was initially created for animals kept in zoos or in laboratories for observation. Cats simply manipulate objects in the circuit board in order to get their food. You can either buy ready-made boards or make one yourself.

You see each cat is unique and special in its own way, and sometimes they can get unpredictable. By doing your part as an owner, you are eliminating possible causes of behavior problems for house cats, such as frustration, boredom, and stress.

Chapter Four: Bringing Home Your Turkish Van Cat

Not a lot of cat owners know how important it is to stimulate cats mentally and physically, and so they, too, become problematic when their pet cat starts destroying furniture, being loud or vocal at night, being aggressive, or worse, getting sick. All of these things can be avoided by being aware of your cat's need to express their natural behaviors. The amount of time a cat will finally feel comfortable in its new home varies according to its past experiences and personality. Giving a cat ample time to adjust to a new home will be beneficial both for you and your pet.

Introducing Your Turkish Van to Other Household Pets

One thing more difficult than introducing a new cat to humans is introducing it to other pets because it's not easy controlling animal behavior, much less, decoding their thoughts and understanding what they're trying to say. You can expect that one pet of yours will always try to dominate your new cat, as animals are territorial in nature. Give them

Chapter Four: Bringing Home Your Turkish Van Cat

time to meet the new member of the family and extend your patience and trust the process.

An older cat is likely to accept another adult cat much easier than it is to like new kittens at once. It will be best to separate the resident cats from the new cat upon arrival, so that you can manage their initial encounter. If you have more than one resident cat at home, introduce them to the new cat individually. It's not necessary to have the cats spend time together immediately. Check out the following tips:

- Keep the cat in its temporary room until it feels confident enough to roam around.
- Keep an eye out for when your cats see each other for the first time. Make sure that they keep a distance to prevent aggression, as first impressions indeed last.
- If there will be no signs of hostility among the cats in the coming days, you may now let them spend time together without a worry.

Chapter Four: Bringing Home Your Turkish Van Cat

When it comes to introducing your cat to your dog/s, keep in mind that meeting a resident dog may be a scary experience for your Turkish Van cat. We highly recommend that you keep your dog confined or in a leash upon the arrival of the new cat. Make sure that the cat's initial base is not accessible to the dog to prevent it from cornering of chasing the cat, even if it only wants to play. Do not let your dog frighten the cat by showing signs of aggression or intimidating the cat by barking. Give your cat and dog enough time to get to know each other by not forcing interaction. Do not leave them alone together unsupervised if you are not sure yet whether they like each other or not.

Chapter Five: Supplies and Nutrition for Turkish Van Cats

Just like other household pets, cats have their own needs too including a place to sleep, bowls to eat in, and fun time. Preparing these before their arrival will save you much time and effort. It will also allow you to find the best ones for them with your budget. You see, any type of pet you intend to keep will definitely cost you additional expenses. However, the price to pay is usually no match for the happiness of owning a pet. Turkish Van cats are low maintenance, but that doesn't mean you can maintain them

Chapter Five: Supplies and Nutritional Turkish Van Cats

without extra effort! As a responsible pet owner, it is your task to know the ideal environment for this breed to keep them feeling happy and secure in your home.

After you've provided all the "cat essentials," the next thing to keep in mind is their nutrition. Maintaining proper nutrition for your Turkish Van is one of the most important yet complex aspects of cat ownership. Oftentimes, keepers don't understand how much diet affects a cat's behavior, health, and even longevity. Never neglect proper feeding schedules and amounts of water intake. As a responsible keeper, it's your duty to make sure that their food intake is controlled. Proper nutrition for this breed is essential for their overall health and heart development. There are certain types of food that can be good and bad for them.

This chapter will cover all the basic essentials that your Turkish Van needs as well as the nutritional guidelines to keep your pet Turkish Van in its optimal health.

Chapter Five: Supplies and Nutritional Turkish Van Cats Kitty Essentials

Cat Patios

Cat patios are structures that provide protection for your cat especially if they are staying outdoors. This is a perfect solution for your cat to enjoy the sights and sounds of the world outside while keeping it safe. If you're having second thoughts about allowing your cat outdoors, building a cat patio will provide the "outside world" that it needs. In addition to that it will also provide benefits such as reduction of veterinary bills due to contracted illnesses and injuries from the outdoors, and it will also give your cat a healthier lifestyle because it can do sunbathing, watch birds, have exercise opportunities, and inhale fresh air. Cat patios also lessen indoor odors by providing another litter box in the enclosure and it can also help reduce the free - roaming cat population in the neighborhood.

Setting up an enclosure entails your time, effort, and additional costs. You can either hire a builder and designer, or you can Do – It – Yourself (DIY). You can check available supplies with your local hardware store and start building.

Chapter Five: Supplies and Nutritional Turkish Van Cats

Some of the basic things you'll need include the following:

- Galvanized wire
- Lumber for framing
- Wire mesh or polycarbonate panels

Consider the following factors if you want a DIY cat patio:

o Find a spot that you cat can easily access like a door, an existing window or a patio where you can build a cat door. You need to also make sure that the location you choose won't be too warm because exposure to direct sunlight during the hottest periods of the day could be harmful to your Turkish Van. You also need to be able to access the enclosure for cleaning and maintenance purposes.

o Make sure to consider the age and condition of your pet. This will help you decide what type of furniture you need to install in the enclosure. Ramps are also ideal for Turkish Van cats.

Chapter Five: Supplies and Nutritional Turkish Van Cats

- o Bigger or more elaborate enclosures could look nice, but keep in mind that you'll be having other expenses for food, grooming, supplies, and vet visits which mean you need to consider your budget so that you won't blow all of it on an enclosure.

Bedding and Cat Furniture

Any kitten or cat will absolutely like anything soft. You may opt for a pillow or a cat bed. Consider the size of your cat when buying bedding. A bed that is too large might leave your pet feeling unsettled. On the other hand, a bed that is too small will ultimately be uncomfortable. As for the cat furniture, you should provide scratch posts or pads, cat trees or something that can provide an outlet for their jumping instincts. These types of furniture will allow your cat to express their natural behaviors such as leaving marks on their territory and climbing. Costs depend on the type you want, but cat furniture prices usually start at around $20 while the price of bedding may vary depending on the size, quality, brands, or design you prefer.

Chapter Five: Supplies and Nutritional Turkish Van Cats

Food and Water Bowls

The best type of bowls especially if you acquired a Turkish Van kitten is the shallow ones because it allows easy access to their food and water. There are many types of bowls to choose from, and plastic is the most popular. However, this material is known to retain smells that the cat may find foul and may discourage them from finishing their food. In some cases, cats that are allergic to plastic end up having a type of cat acne on their chin. The most recommended type of food bowl is stainless steel because it is sturdy and generally harmless for cats. Steel bowls are often dishwasher safe, which could help busy owners save time.

Make sure to keep the food bowls clean and rinse them regularly to prevent the build-up of bacteria. It will cost you around $3 for a single bowl and around $6 for a set of 2 bowls.

Chapter Five: Supplies and Nutritional Turkish Van Cats

Litter Box

Depending on your cat's personality, you can either choose a hooded litter box from privacy or a plain plastic tray for those who don't enjoy feeling boxed. Cats tend to do their potty business in the same areas, unlike dogs that need to be walked until they find an ideal area. This is why you need to get your cat a litter box.

There a lot of types if litter boxes depending on your budget and your preferences. There is even an automated poop handler that could do the dirty work for you. There are various types of cat litter such as clumping and non – clumping clay, wheat, recycled paper, grass, corn – based litter, walnut shells (crushed), gel crystals to name a few. The most common type of litter available in the groceries is clumping-cat litter; it is highly - absorbent, although it tends to be a bit dusty. The cost of cat litter usually starts at $15.

You need to also make sure that you maintain your cat's litter box. What you can do is fill it up with about 2 to 3 inches so that your pet can dig through it and learn to cover its waste. Make sure to scoop out the waste at least twice a

Chapter Five: Supplies and Nutritional Turkish Van Cats

day. Some cats would not use a soiled litter box so in order to prevent them from doing their business elsewhere, ensure to keep their litter tray clean. Dispose the soiled litter properly by putting it in an appropriate garbage bag. Avoid using their poop as fertilizer because it will surely attract other cats, flies, insects etc.

Physically and Mentally Stimulating Toys

Stock up on toys so that you and your family can bond with your pet. Playtime is very important for a kitten's development and it can be therapeutic for humans too. You can buy any type of cat toy you wish, just remember to avoid buying those with parts than can cause choking or strangling. There are a lot of cheap cat toys in the stores and online, so you don't have to worry about spending much on them. What you can do is to get a couple of them and rotate it so that your cat will not get bored easily with it. It's also best to consider what kind of toy your pet prefers.

Chapter Five: Supplies and Nutritional Turkish Van Cats

Nutritional Needs of Cats

Feline pets just like humans also need a healthy diet to thrive. Feeding your Turkish Van cat the wrong food could definitely lead to a health disaster. Knowing the proper amount needed by your pet is best determined by your veterinarian. If you've already bought some cat food but are not sure if it is good for your cat, bring the cat food to your vet to have its nutritional values assessed. Cats whether they are kittens or adults need a balance amount of minerals, vitamins, protein, enzymes, fatty acids and water.

First stop is the most important of all – water. Cats have low levels of thirst because they can fulfill much of their water requirements by eating fresh, raw food. This is why cats that eat dry food often have more health issues than those who eat wet cat food. Cats that lack water in their body end up getting dehydrated and usually have urine that is too concentrated. Make sure to always prepare fresh and clean drinking water for your pet. And if ever you feel that they are not drinking enough, you can get cat drinking fountains that mimic the experience of drinking from running water.

Every cat needs a great amount of protein in their body. Your pet can get a good supply of this from meat since plant sources do not supply Taurine which is an essential amino acid that cats need. If your cat lacks Taurine, this can lead to health issues so make sure to include protein - rich food in their diet. Another important nutrient is vitamins. It is important to household pets as it is for us humans. Vitamins provide good metabolism and also contributes to normal growth and bodily functions.

Another important nutrient that your cat needs on a daily basis is essential fatty acids. This nutrient can't be gain from plant sources, which again justifies why a cat's diet needs to be composed of meat. These nutrients are involved with metabolism functions and cell integrity in a cat's body. Another essential is antioxidants and enzymes can be found in healthy food sources for cats as these can help protect their body from free radicals that can damage the cells.

Chapter Five: Supplies and Nutritional Turkish Van Cats

Last but not the least are minerals are involved in most of a cat's physiological reactions like enzyme formulation, oxygen transportation, and nutrient utilization. The following minerals are needed by cats on a daily basis:

- Chloride
- Chromium
- Copper
- Calcium
- Cobalt
- Iodine
- Iron
- Zinc
- Magnesium
- Manganese
- Potassium

Feeding Requirements

Feeding your pet dry cat food is okay, as long as it is balanced. It could be better to ration the food rather than to free - feed. If your cat only eats dry food, make sure to encourage it to drink much water to avoid developing kidney stones. On the other hand wet food or canned food is always a good choice, but make sure to exercise control over the amount your cat eats since this type of food is more palatable than dry food, this can cause our cat to overeat. According to veterinarians, mixing dry and wet food to make meals more appealing is not bad. However, you got to make sure that you don't go over the ideal calorie intake of your cat. Make sure to consult your vet for the right amount of food intake.

Toxic Foods for Cats

Take note of the following human foods that are toxic to cats in general:

- Chocolates and drinks (especially with caffeine)
- Dairy products such as butter and milk
- Garlic
- Onion
- Raw dough
- Alcohol
- Raisins
- Grapes
- Dog food

Chapter Five: Supplies and Nutritional Turkish Van Cats

When it comes to frequency of meals, you'd be surprised to know that kittens need more food for development than adult cats. Usually, kittens up to 6 months of age may require being fed 3 meals per day, while most cats over 6 months of age will do fine with just 2 meals per day. Once your cat reaches 7 years old, you may feed them once a day and maintain that routine.

Homemade Meal Options

Homemade food is an option by pet owners to make sure that the cat will have adequate water and you will have full control over all of the things you will put there. On the other hand, if you are a very busy person, the conventional commercial premium food is often convenient and often cheaper. The choice heavily relies on your preference. However, if you give raw meat, the risk is that meat might contain parasites that will be harmful to your pet's body. On the other hand, cooked meat will lose some of its nutrients because of the processing. We highly recommend that you could try a combination of the two.

Chapter Five: Supplies and Nutritional Turkish Van Cats

Chapter Six: Official Breed Standard and Showing Your Cat

The Turkish Van is indeed a great cat to have around the house because of its unique traits and amazing personality. It is also a joy to show it off to friends and family but do you know that you can officially "brag" to everyone including other cat breeds? Turkish Van keepers have a strong desire to share their cat's well – built body as well as its intelligent and independent disposition to the rest of the world of cat fanciers. Now you can do the same too! However, you need to ensure that your pet follows the

Chapter Six: Official Breed Standard and Showing Your Cat

official breed standard which can slightly vary depending on the cat organization that you're going to sign up your pet into. You need to also learn a few things about the process and training involved before you and your cat joins any show competition so that you'll be sure that your Turkish Van is qualified and ready to crush the competition!

Official Breed Standard

Below are the general breed standards for the Turkish Van cat:

Head (30 points)

  Shape (18 points)

- Chin
- Nose
- Profile
- Cheekbones
- Boning

Ears (7 points)

- Shape
- Size

Chapter Six: Official Breed Standard and Showing Your Cat

- Placement

Eyes (5 points)

- Shape
- Size
- Placement

Body (30 points)

Type (18 points)

- Muscle
- Boning
- Size
- Length

Legs and Feet (5 points)

Tail (7 points)

Coat (15 points)

Color and Pattern (20 points)

Balance (5 points)

General: The Turkish Van cat is a naturally rugged breed that ranges in climatically remote regions in the Middle East

Chapter Six: Official Breed Standard and Showing Your Cat

specifically in Turkey. The breed is known for its "Van" pattern which is a very unique and distinct markings and coat coloration on its head and tail. The Van pattern has also been adopted by various cat breeds to describe white cats with markings on the head and tail.

The Turkish Van is a semi – long – haired cat that has a solid body built and possesses a great breadth to the chest. The power and strength of this breed is shown on the substantiality of its legs and overall body. It takes around 3 to 5 years for the Turkish Van breed to reach full development and maturity which is why allowances must be made for their sex and age.

This cat breed is very alert, clever, independent, secure, and knows how to balance himself using its four feet on a solid surface.

Balance:

The cat should convey an impression of a well – balanced and well – proportion physicality.

No physical feature should be exaggerated that fosters either extremes or weaknesses.

Chapter Six: Official Breed Standard and Showing Your Cat

Head:

- The head should be broad wedge.
- It should gentle contours
- It should possess a medium – length nose that goes along its big and muscular body structure
- The ears shouldn't be included in the wedge
- Must possess prominent cheekbones
- When it comes to profile, the cat's nose should have a slight dip below its eye level marked by a change in the direction of their hair.
- Allowances should be made for jowling especially in male cats
- The cat should possess a rounded muzzle and a firm chin that aligns with the upper lip and its nose

Ears:

- Ears must be proportionate to the body
- It must be moderately large
- It should be set relatively high and set well apart
- The inside edge of the ear should be slightly angled to the outside with the outside edge

Chapter Six: Official Breed Standard and Showing Your Cat

relatively straight but not necessarily align with its side of the face.

- The ears should be wide at the base and the tips should be slightly rounded while the inside must be well – feathered.

Eyes:

- The eyes should preferably be moderately large
- It should be rounded and the aperture must be slightly drawn out at the corners.
- The eyes must also be equidistant from the outside base of the cat's ear to the tip of the nose.
- It must be set at a slant
- It should be alert, expressive, and clear

Body:

- The body should be sturdy, muscular, relatively long, deep – chested and broad
- Mature Turkish Van males should sport a marked muscular development particularly in its neck and shoulders.

Chapter Six: Official Breed Standard and Showing Your Cat

- Its shoulders should be at least as broad as its head.
- The shoulders must also flow into the cat's ribcage, hip and pelvic region.
- For males, they should be substantially larger than their counterparts and should sport much greater body development.

Legs and Feet:

- The legs should be muscular and moderately long
- They should be set wide apart and taper to rounded relatively large feet.
- The legs and feet must be proportionate to the body.
- There should be five toes in front, and four toes behind

Tail:

- The tail should be long but must be proportionate with its body.
- It should possess a brush appearance

Chapter Six: Official Breed Standard and Showing Your Cat

- The hair length on the tail is the same with the length of the cat's semi – long coat.

Coat:

- The coat must be semi – long and it should have a cashmere – like texture
- It should be soft to the roots with no trace of undercoat
- There would be allowances for the coat lengths of the breed since they've originated from extreme climate conditions.
- The summer coat should be short and it should sport an appearance of a shorthair while the winter coat should be thick and long.
- There should be a feathering on the cat's ears, feet, belly, and legs. And the facial fur must be short.
- The frontal neck ruff and the tail brush become more pronounced as the cat's age.

Color and Pattern:

- The Van Pattern only glistens on a chalk – white colored body. It also has colored marking on the head and the tail

Chapter Six: Official Breed Standard and Showing Your Cat

- One or more random marking up to the color on 15% of the cat's body are allowed (except the tail and head color).
- Random markings shouldn't be of a number or size to detract from the Van pattern that could make the breed appear bi – color.
- A desirable color and pattern is one that's symmetrical to the head markings that are divided by white up to the level of the ears' front edge.

Penalty:

- If there's any evidence toward extremes such as fine – boning, svelte or short cobbiness.
- If there's greater white in the tail (or around 20%) and has a flat profile.

Disqualify:

- Total absence of color in the area from the cat's eye level up to the back of its tail or head.
- If it has a definite nose break

Chapter Six: Official Breed Standard and Showing Your Cat

- If there are skeletal or genetic defects such as kinked/ abnormal tail, flat ribcage, incorrect number of toes or crossed eyes.
- If the color is in excess of 15% of the cat's body, except the tail and head color.

Turkish Van Colors

Eye Color: Applicable to all coat colors. Take note that the eye color fades with age

- Amber
- Blue
- Odd – Eyed

Nose Leather: Applicable to all coat colors.

- Pink

Paw Pads: Applicable to all coat colors.

- Pink is preferred
- Color spots on paw pads are also acceptable due to the 2 colors in the pattern

Chapter Six: Official Breed Standard and Showing Your Cat

For Solid and White Colors

- **Red:** Ranges from warm red to deep auburn. It must be one level of shade and sound to the roots.
- **Cream:** Must have one level shade of buff cream and should also be sound to the roots.
- **Black:** Must be dense coal black that's free of any tinge of rust on its tips. Must be sound to the roots
- **Blue:** Must be one level tone of blue and sound to the roots

For Tabby and White Colors

Tabby markings are clearly defined and dense. The amount of tabby markings depends on the size as well as its placement on the cat's body and head spots. A spot could be the size that only ground color is seen which is why it may not be enough color to determine if it's a mackerel or classic marking.

- **Red Tabby:** Ground color creamy red. The markings range from warm red to deep auburn
- **Cream Tabby:** Ground color very pale cream. The markings of buff cream should be darker than the

Chapter Six: Official Breed Standard and Showing Your Cat

ground color in order to afford good contrast though it should remain within the diluted range.

- **Brown Tabby:** Ground color creamy beige. The markings are dense black.
- **Blue Tabby:** Ground color pale bluish ivory. The markings should be a deep blue in order to afford a good contrast with its ground color. Warm patina or fawn over the colored portions.

Parti – Color and White Colors

- **Tortoiseshell:** Black and red patches with tabby markings are allowed in the red portion.
- **Dilute Tortoiseshell:** Blue and cream patches with tabby markings are allowed in the cream portion,
- **Brown Patched Tabby:** Brown tabby description with patches of red tabby or red
- **Blue Patched Tabby:** Blue tabby description with patches of cream tabby or cream.

Chapter Six: Official Breed Standard and Showing Your Cat

Showing Your Turkish Van

In cat shows, judges compare cats to breed standards. These standards state how an ideal Turkish Van cat looks and behaves. Cats score higher when they are able to fulfill more breed standards set by the organizer so make sure that you follow the official breed standards mentioned in the previous section. Breed standards are accurate, yet flexible. According to the Cat Fanciers Association, the given standards aim to describe features that come from the natural style of the breed, but at times, judges also consider the proportion of the cat's overall features rather than whether they exactly conform to the measurements stated. You can sign up your pet for either a specialty cat shows or an all – breed cat shows. The former is a competition where cats compete within a particular breed or color divisions while the latter is a show that competes with other cat breeds and not just among Turkish Van.

In the CFA, separate shows run simultaneously throughout a hall, with rings for each judge. The process

Chapter Six: Official Breed Standard and Showing Your Cat

involves keepers finding their designated cage numbers and waiting to be called. Once the number is called, you can bring your pet to the cages in the different rings where the judges can inspect and rate them. Don't worry because ring clerks and ring stewards are there to help you out, records are maintained and cages are kept clean. Each judge is also accompanied by a master clerk. After examining all the cats in the all - breed or specialty shows, the judges will then tally the scores and present the top 10 cats. As for the recognition and awarding, there are 1st, 2nd, and 3rd placers but when a cat obtains six ribbons in the open category, it is declared as the champion and proceeds to compete with other champions. Depending on the organization, champion cats that earn 200 points will be declared as the grand champion.

Training Your Turkish Van for Show

One important thing to keep in mind is not be harsh when you are training your pet. Sure be competitive but not to the point where you will punish your cat if he/ she doesn't cooperate with you. What you can do is use rewards to

Chapter Six: Official Breed Standard and Showing Your Cat

encourage your cat during training time and always be patient to obtain desirable behavior. Cat show judges inspect not only how your entry looks, but also how it behaves and responds. Training your pet Turkish Van before a show could be of great help in earning better scores in the judges' books.

One of the first things you need to teach your cat is to stand erect with a good posture. Although it is more difficult to teach cats to sit and stand than dogs, try to train your pet to do these for a few moments. The judges will be impressed. Reward your cat with gentle nose strokes downward whenever it is in good posture. Or you can also ask an expert to train your cat prior to a show. You can also check out the mentorship program of the CFA where newbie keepers can be accustomed to the process in cat shows. Make sure to play with your cat and offer it treats to keep it as happy and relaxed as possible especially during the show. You can also choose to bring your cat out to a show even if he/she isn't joining yet, so that your Turkish Van will be familiar with the sights and sounds of the event.

Chapter Six: Official Breed Standard and Showing Your Cat

Below are other training tips that your cat needs to get used to:

Get your cat used to being carried around. Your pet needs to get used to being carried on your forearms and hands. This can be a bit tricky for Turkish Van cats because they don't want to be carried around much unlike other cat breeds but the earlier you start carrying them comfortably, the better they will feel once the show day arrives.

Make your Turkish Van confident by placing them on unfamiliar surfaces. This can include a desk or even on the grooming table. Play with them to make them feel confident being in these surfaces. You can also find a toy that your pet likes and teach it to jump up to touch the toy.

Keep your pet socialized. Make sure to constantly introduce and socialize your pet to new people and friends so that it does not develop a shy or easily frightened attitude.

Chapter Seven: Health Care for Turkish Van Cats

The health of your Turkish Van cat is perhaps the most important thing you need to focus on because this will give you benefits in the long run. Think about it, if your pet is healthy, you don't need to pay for medical bills and you will also save time and effort of constantly taking vet trips. You will also save your cat from pain and you're going to lessen the risk of them catching any major illnesses. However, keep in mind that good health comes with a price. You need to provide the needed vaccines, spay/neuter them,

Chapter Seven: Health Care for Turkish Van Cats

maintain their hygiene through grooming and go for vet routine checkups to ensure that your cat is at its best health.

Vaccines and Vet Exams

As costly as it may sound, you need to vaccine your cat especially when you got it in a very young stage. Remember, the mother may have given antibodies to prevent common diseases, but these are not enough. Your cat needs additional protection against common ailments.

At around six to eight weeks old, core vaccines are needed, especially for feline distemper, feline calicivirus, and feline rhinotracheitis. You also need to ask your vet if you need to have a vaccine against chlamydia. The core vaccines must be given every three to four weeks, and the final kitten vaccinations should be given at 14 to 16 weeks of age. At around ten to twelve weeks old, second vaccinations of the core vaccines are required. You may also ask your vet about the feline leukaemia. Then when your pet hits twelve to sixteen weeks old you should already have your pet

Chapter Seven: Health Care for Turkish Van Cats

rabies shot. Third round of vaccination of core vaccines are needed for fourteen to sixteen weeks old kittens.

As for vet exams, they usually like to perform the examination in their own ways, especially with the parts that they are examining. It doesn't matter where they begin, as long as they will examine everything. Remember, this vet examination is done every time you go to the vet. When you schedule your pet for a vet exam, what you can do to help during the process is to calm down your Turkish Van or keep him/her quiet during a physical examination, especially when the vet is using a stethoscope. Talking during the examination will lead to interruption of your vet's concentration and could interfere with the thoroughness.

You can also ask questions and suggestions after the cat's examination. Questions like if you need to examine your cat at home, what signs are you looking for when examining the cat, how to tell if your cat is overweight or underweight, and what solutions can be done to alleviate the health issue if any can be helpful for you.

Chapter Seven: Health Care for Turkish Van Cats

Spaying and Neutering

When it comes to spaying and neutering your pet, vets strongly suggest that owners spay or neuter their cats. Neutering is found to have a lot of benefits including the correction of bad behavior such as territorial spraying, aggression, and roaming, which are common for male cats. Female cats can also be observed to have better behavior after surgery. If they are spayed between three to six months, you could protect them from mammary cancer and from an infection of the uterus which usually affects older female cats.

Operations at full - service vet clinics may cost you around $200 for a male cat, and $300 up to $500 for a female cat at the time of this writing. For non - profit spay or neuter services, they could charge as low as $50, and may vary according to your location. Only licensed veterinarians are allowed to perform these surgeries. You can check out the website of The American Society for the Prevention of Cruelty to Animals and Humane Society because they list low-cost spays and neuter programs for owners' reference.

Chapter Seven: Health Care for Turkish Van Cats

Grooming Your Turkish Van

Proper grooming is essential in order to maintain your Turkish Van's luxurious water – resistant coat, and overall well-being. Although cats in general can clean themselves well, you still have to take them on trips to a trusted groomer to make sure that they are in top shape.

If you want to maintain your pet's coat, you should comb and not just brush it by running your fingers through its coat to prevent matting – although you won't have much problem since the coat of the Turkish Van cat is not prone to matting.

Part of grooming practices is to check your pet's ear for foul odor and dirt build-up. They can usually clean this area by themselves, but you can help them by using a damp cotton ball and gently rubbing inside to collect dirt and debris. A cat with clean ears is a healthy cat.

As what we've mentioned in previous chapters, Turkish Van cats love to swim but it doesn't translate to them enjoying taking baths just like other cat breeds. Your

Chapter Seven: Health Care for Turkish Van Cats

pet doesn't need much bathing. However, you can still give them a quick shower once a week in the tub. In addition to bathing, brushing its teeth is also important. Consult with a vet for your cat's dental health.

All breeds of cats are susceptible to dental problems, but you can minimize the risk of acquiring it with regular brushing. Last but not least is nail – trimming. You need to trim your Turkish Van's nails as this will prevent your cat from accidentally wounding both you and other animal companions. It can also help prevent damage on your home furniture. If you are not confident trimming its nails yourself, you may take your pet to a groomer and have it done there to avoid wounding its paws.

Chapter Seven: Health Care for Turkish Van Cats

Glossary of Cat Terms

Abundism – Referring to a cat that has markings more prolific than is normal.

Acariasis – A type of mite infection.

ACF – Australian Cat Federation

Affix – A cattery name that follows the cat's registered name; cattery owner, not the breeder of the cat.

Agouti – A type of natural coloring pattern in which individual hairs have bands of light and dark coloring.

Ailurophile – A person who loves cats.

Albino – A type of genetic mutation which results in little to no pigmentation, in the eyes, skin, and coat.

Allbreed – Referring to a show that accepts all breeds or a judge who is qualified to judge all breeds.

Alley Cat – A non-pedigreed cat.

Alter – A desexed cat; a male cat that has been neutered or a female that has been spayed.

Amino Acid – The building blocks of protein; there are 22 types for cats, 11 of which can be synthesized and 11 which must come from the diet (see essential amino acid).

Anestrus – The period between estrus cycles in a female cat.

Chapter Seven: Health Care for Turkish Van Cats

Any Other Variety (AOV) – A registered cat that doesn't conform to the breed standard.

ASH – American Shorthair, a breed of cat.

Back Cross – A type of breeding in which the offspring is mated back to the parent.

Balance – Referring to the cat's structure; proportional in accordance with the breed standard.

Barring – Describing the tabby's striped markings.

Base Color – The color of the coat.

Bicolor – A cat with patched color and white.

Blaze – A white coloring on the face, usually in the shape of an inverted V.

Bloodline – The pedigree of the cat.

Brindle – A type of coloring, a brownish or tawny coat with streaks of another color.

Castration – The surgical removal of a male cat's testicles.

Cat Show – An event where cats are shown and judged.

Cattery – A registered cat breeder; also, a place where cats may be boarded.

CFA – The Cat Fanciers Association.

Cobby – A compact body type.

Chapter Seven: Health Care for Turkish Van Cats

Colony – A group of cats living wild outside.

Color Point – A type of coat pattern that is controlled by color point alleles; pigmentation on the tail, legs, face, and ears with an ivory or white coat.

Colostrum – The first milk produced by a lactating female; contains vital nutrients and antibodies.

Conformation – The degree to which a pedigreed cat adheres to the breed standard.

Cross Breed – The offspring produced by mating two distinct breeds.

Dam – The female parent.

Declawing – The surgical removal of the cat's claw and first toe joint.

Developed Breed – A breed that was developed through selective breeding and crossing with established breeds.

Down Hairs – The short, fine hairs closest to the body which keep the cat warm.

DSH – Domestic Shorthair.

Estrus – The reproductive cycle in female cats during which she becomes fertile and receptive to mating.

Fading Kitten Syndrome – Kittens that die within the first two weeks after birth; the cause is generally unknown.

Feral – A wild, untamed cat of domestic descent.

Chapter Seven: Health Care for Turkish Van Cats

Gestation – Pregnancy; the period during which the fetuses develop in the female's uterus.

Guard Hairs – Coarse, outer hairs on the coat.

Harlequin – A type of coloring in which there are van markings of any color with the addition of small patches of the same color on the legs and body.

Inbreeding – The breeding of related cats within a closed group or breed.

Kibble – Another name for dry cat food.

Lilac – A type of coat color that is pale pinkish-gray.

Line – The pedigree of ancestors; family tree.

Litter – The name given to a group of kittens born at the same time from a single female.

Mask – A type of coloring seen on the face in some breeds.

Matts – Knots or tangles in the cat's fur.

Mittens – White markings on the feet of a cat.

Moggie – Another name for a mixed breed cat.

Mutation – A change in the DNA of a cell.

Muzzle – The nose and jaws of an animal.

Natural Breed – A breed that developed without selective breeding or the assistance of humans.

Chapter Seven: Health Care for Turkish Van Cats

Neutering – Desexing a male cat.

Open Show – A show in which spectators are allowed to view the judging.

Pads – The thick skin on the bottom of the feet.

Particolor – A type of coloration in which there are markings of two or more distinct colors.

Patched – A type of coloration in which there is any solid color, tabby, or tortoiseshell color plus white.

Pedigree – A purebred cat; the cat's papers showing its family history.

Pet Quality – A cat that is not deemed of high enough standard to be shown or bred.

Piebald – A cat with white patches of fur.

Points – Also color points; markings of contrasting color on the face, ears, legs, and tail.

Pricked – Referring to ears that sit upright.

Purebred – A pedigreed cat.

Queen – An intact female cat.

Roman Nose – A type of nose shape with a bump or arch.

Scruff – The loose skin on the back of a cat's neck.

Selective Breeding – A method of modifying or improving a breed by choosing cats with desirable traits.

Chapter Seven: Health Care for Turkish Van Cats

Senior – A cat that is more than 5 but less than 7 years old.

Sire – The male parent of a cat.

Solid – Also self; a cat with a single coat color.

Spay – Desexing a female cat.

Stud – An intact male cat.

Tabby – A type of coat pattern consisting of a contrasting color over a ground color.

Tom Cat – An intact male cat.

Tortoiseshell – A type of coat pattern consisting of a mosaic of red or cream and another base color.

Tri-Color – A type of coat pattern consisting of three distinct colors in the coat.

Tuxedo – A black and white cat.

Unaltered – A cat that has not been desexed.

Index

A

accessories	23, 26, 36, 43, 44, 48, 107
active	35, 40
adopt	36
adopting	2
age	5, 20, 25, 61, 88, 109
alfalfa	52, 61, 62, 63, 113, 114
altered	20
angora	3
antibiotics	98, 102
antiseptic	26, 72, 76
appearance	3

B

baby	5, 7, 34, 35, 36, 40, 41, 42, 61, 64, 69, 100
back	6, 54, 77, 89, 107
bacteria	24, 46, 50, 76, 101, 106
bathing	71, 74
bed	23
bedding	27, 28, 45, 48, 50, 68, 94, 105, 107, 108, 131
behavior	66, 92
belly	5, 67
birth	5, 6, 61, 68
birthing	5
bladder	96
bleach	107
blood	6, 75, 94, 95
body	4, 6, 7, 41, 54, 75, 80, 99, 104
bodyweight	27, 58, 59, 62, 114
bowls	23, 24, 48
box	5, 6, 26, 30, 41, 46, 67, 68, 69, 96, 113
breathing	94, 103

breed 2, 4, 5, 8, 18, 23, 25, 27, 29, 30, 33, 34, 35, 44, 48, 65, 66, 70, 79, 80, 87, 88, 92, 115
breed standard 79, 81
breeder 33, 34, 35, 40
breeding 2, 5, 24, 34, 35, 36, 65, 66
breeds 3, 4, 20, 21, 24, 35, 71, 74, 80
broken 4
brush 26, 72, 74, 88
budget 25, 26, 29

C

cage 20, 24, 26, 28, 36, 41, 43, 45, 46, 47, 48, 51, 54, 66, 67, 96, 97, 99, 104, 106, 107, 112, 115
care 30, 75, 92, 129, 131
cat litter 50
cats 21, 25, 30, 108
causes 93, 96, 99
characteristics 3
chest 54
chewing 44
children 2, 5, 31
chin 4
cleaning 88
clipping 23
coat 3, 4, 5, 6, 7, 4, 14, 71, 72, 75, 99, 105, 111
collar 26
coloring 3
colors 4
comb 72
condition 6, 35, 72, 94, 96, 99, 105
conjunctivitis 101
convulsions 94, 100
costs 23, 26, 27, 28
courtship 66

D

dangerous 21, 47, 102

defecate 51
diagnosis 92, 99
diarrhea 40
diet 2, 27, 30, 47, 57, 59, 61, 63, 69, 77, 92, 114, 131
digestion 57, 60
discharge 41, 101, 103
diseases 47, 93, 106, 108, 129
disinfect 104, 107
disorientation 101
docile 21, 30
doe 5, 66, 67, 68, 69, 115
dogs 21, 25, 30, 108

E

ears 3, 41, 71, 75, 95, 101, 108, 115
embryos 67, 115
energy 5
exercise 5, 43, 44, 46, 112
export 19
eyes 41

F

feeding 60, 69
female 4, 20, 66, 67, 114
fever 75, 93, 94, 95, 103
fiber 19, 50, 57, 58, 61, 77, 113
fluid 98, 103
food 4, 6, 7, 23, 24, 27, 28, 48, 60, 77, 89, 94, 98, 107, 113
fruit 59, 62, 114

G

games 44
genes 6
grooming 4, 6, 23, 26, 28, 30, 71, 72, 75, 88, 89, 106
grooming tools 72

guard hairs 3, 4, 6, 7

H

habitat 2, 44, 106
hair 3, 6, 68, 69, 96, 104
handling 43
head 3, 7, 76, 100, 101, 104
head tilt 100, 101
health 2, 27, 34, 35, 71
health problems 2, 92, 93
healthy 27, 28, 33, 35, 40, 58, 63, 69, 106, 114
history 33
hutch 24

I

illness 41, 92, 105, 106
import 19
inbreeding 67
incisors 76
infection 76, 95, 96, 98, 101, 102, 103, 105
infectious 93, 101
inflammation 41, 93, 96, 97, 102
information 33, 34
initial costs 23
intact 4
intelligent 4, 15, 112

J

judging 89

K

kindling 5, 70, 115
kittens 115

L

leafy greens 58, 114
legs 4, 6, 7, 104
lesions 99, 104
lethargic 41
lethargy 94, 95, 103
license 18, 19, 33
lifespan 5
litter 4, 26, 27, 28, 30, 32, 36, 40, 43, 46, 49, 51, 52, 64, 68, 69, 96, 113, 131

M

male 4, 6, 20, 66, 114, 115
malnutrition 104
marking 3, 66
materials 24, 46
mating 66, 67, 68
mats 74
meat 5, 7, 19
medications 103, 104
microchipping 23
milk 6, 61, 62, 70, 114, 115
mites 105, 108

N

nails 6, 71, 75
neck 6, 105
nervous 21
nest 5, 6, 68, 69, 113
nesting box 68, 69
neuter 23
neutered 25
noise 7, 47, 112
nose 4
nutrients 57, 58, 61, 69
nutrition 4

nutritional needs 57

O

offspring 4, 6
organization 3, 87
outdoor 47, 112

P

pair 20, 66, 77
palpate 67
parasites 47, 96, 106, 108
pattern 6
permit 18, 19
pet 27, 41
pet store 33, 35
pets 5, 7, 14, 18, 19, 21, 53, 111, 129
play 41
pregnancy 66
pregnant 5, 6, 67
prize 89
probiotics 102
problems 42
pros and cons 29
protein 58, 61, 113
purchase 23, 26, 34, 40, 57, 113

Q

qualifications 80
quick 75

R

rabies 19
recovery 93

registration 34
regulations 18, 19, 87
reproductive 101
requirements 44
respiratory 101

S

sanitation 96, 97, 99, 102, 104
scent 4
schedule 67, 88, 108
scissors 72
self 89
selling 4, 19
shedding 6, 74
shoulders 3, 6
show 7, 24, 72, 80, 87, 88, 89, 92, 94
showing 2, 79
signs 41
size 7, 20, 27, 45
skin 3, 97, 98, 105, 108
sneezing 101, 103
social 20
socialization 5
solid 7
spay 23
spayed 18, 25, 36
standard 80
stimulation 5, 44
stress 104, 105, 106
supplies 23, 26
surgery 23
swollen 42
symptoms 92, 93, 94, 99, 100, 103

T

tail 6, 105
taming 43

teeth 6, 25, 58, 71, 72, 75, 76, 77
temperament 21
temperature 75
tests 99
texture 6
ticks 95
time 5, 30, 41, 49, 53, 57, 62, 65, 66, 69, 71, 72, 75, 89, 92, 93, 113
tips 32
toxic 60
toys 23, 28, 44
train 26, 51
training 5
treatment 2, 92, 93, 94, 95, 97, 98, 100, 102, 103, 104
type 3, 28, 43, 49, 52, 58, 59, 72, 103
types 43

U

unaltered 4
urinate 51

V

vaccinations 23, 35
vegetables 27, 57, 58, 59, 60, 62, 113, 114, 131
vet. 28
veterinarian 28
veterinary 27
viral 93, 95, 102

W

walk 42
water 23, 24, 48, 57, 88, 89, 94, 98, 107, 113, 114
water bottle 24, 48, 113
weight 63, 94, 103, 114

Photo Credits

Page 1 Photo by user Joe via Flickr.com,

https://www.flickr.com/photos/joetourist/38210643194/

Page 6 Photo by user Inkeri Siltala via Flickr.com,

https://www.flickr.com/photos/100576637@N06/15990094544

Page 20 Photo by user gadgetgirl via Flickr.com,

https://www.flickr.com/photos/gadgetgirl70/5282638470/

Page 35 Photo by user Heikki Siltala via Flickr.com,

https://www.flickr.com/photos/heikkisiltala/6971474634/

Page 44 Photo by user Marcel Oosterwijk via Flickr.com,

https://www.flickr.com/photos/wackelijmrooster/6140601185/

Page 60 Photo by user Inkeri Siltala via Flickr.com,

https://www.flickr.com/photos/100576637@N06/20073838012/

Page 73 Photo by user Inkeri Siltala via Flickr.com,

https://www.flickr.com/photos/100576637@N06/15990092174

Page 89 Photo by user Inkeri Siltala via Flickr.com,

https://www.flickr.com/photos/100576637@N06/15992570563

References

About the Turkish Van - Cat Fanciers Association

http://cfa.org/breeds/breedssthrut/turkishvan.aspx

Turkish Van - Cattime.com

https://cattime.com/cat-breeds/turkish-van-cats#/slide/1

Turkish Van Cats - Purina.co.uk

https://www.purina.co.uk/cats/cat-breeds/library/turkish-van

Turkish Van Cat Breed - TheHappyCatSite.com

https://www.thehappycatsite.com/turkish-van-cat/

Everything You Need to Know About Turkish Van Cats - PrettyLitterCats.com

https://prettylittercats.com/blogs/prettylitter-blog/turkish-van-cats

Turkish Van Cat History and Characteristics - LovetoKnow.com

https://cats.lovetoknow.com/cat-breeds/turkish-van-cat

Turkish Van - Zooplus.co.uk

https://www.zooplus.co.uk/magazine/cat/cat-breeds/turkish-van

What's new, pussycat? It's time for your swim — Turkish Van cats get their own pool - TheTimes.co.uk

https://www.thetimes.co.uk/article/what-s-new-pussycat-it-s-time-for-your-swim-turkish-van-cats-get-their-own-pool-k5jhgmvh5

Turkish Van - RoyalCanin.in

http://www.royalcanin.in/breeds/cat-breeds/turkish-van

Turkish Van Cat Breed - Petwave.com

https://www.petwave.com/Cats/Breeds/Turkish-Van.aspx

Turkish Van Cat Breed Information and Personality Traits - Hillspet.com

https://www.hillspet.com/cat-care/cat-breeds/turkish-van

www.ingramcontent.com/pod-product-compliance
Lightning Source LLC
Chambersburg PA
CBHW060840050426
42453CB00008B/764